Light Calling

Poems

Hope you find one or two things that
you like here, Dorothy.
All the best,
David.

David Masters

DEDICATION
For Anne, Stuart and Ian

'We can touch the noumenal world by touching the phenomenal world deeply.' (Thich Nhat Hanh)

Trembling Spiders' webs
Struggle to stitch together
What's left of summer.

ACKNOWLEDGEMENT

I owe a deep gratitude to my wife, Anne, whose comments and observations have been invaluable. I remain forever grateful that her patience towards me extends far beyond the reading of words.

CONTENTS
(Mostly ordered chronologically)

A KALEIDOSCOPE OF BUTTERFLIES

It was a summer to yearn
For something.
A flash of vivid scarlet in the corner of my eye
Caused my head to quickly turn;
But too late.

A glimpse of bright pattern
Appearing and disappearing between
Green leaves and stalks
Forced my eyes to focus hard
With the concentration of a predator;
Yet it eluded me.

What I thirst for is the warm sun
The bright light
My eyes feasting on patterns
Colours and shapes
Effortlessly formed into a
Silent
Fluttering
Dashing
Flashing
Kaleidoscope of Butterflies.

August 2007

THE INVISIBLE WOUND

Buried
Deep
Out of sight
Where no sympathy is sought
No enquiries are made.

I am drawn
Irresistibly
To that dark place
Both attracted and repelled
By its truth and its lies
Not knowing if it deceives.

Inflamed by my anger and bitterness
Every touch and pull
Keeps it raw
And with a twisted crimson smile it
Mocks my best efforts
To soothe or to heal.

Weary from its gnawing and
Obscure presence
I sink down to
Pray, curse, cry, implore, reason
Trying each in turn
In the hope that anything offered may be
Heard sympathetically.

I wait alone in that dark place
Eyes straining to see if what is
Buried
Deep
Shows any sign of responding.

August 2007

A TILT OF THE HEAD

Above the horizon
The stars pierce the sky
With cool clarity.

Below the horizon
The bush passes frieze-like:
Scorched ground
Twisted trees
A scattering of leaves clutching at life.

Above the horizon
The stars declare themselves in
Stark simplicity.

Below the horizon
A journey is made
The smell of petrol
The rattling and jarring of
Nerves and bodies as the small bus zigzags
Avoiding potholes.

At the horizon two worlds meet
In a necessary but imperfect journey.

A tilt of the head upwards or downwards
Allows my eyes to rest with ease on what is above
And with unease on what is below.

August 2007

ANOTHER TEAR

A hair
Moves on my arm
I feel nothing else
I stand
Motionless
Arms folded
Head bowed
Another tear
Slips from my cheek
And falls
A hair
Moves on my arm
I feel nothing else.

August 2007

AFTER YVES KLEIN

A painting of figures
Held there as if in a moment of dance
Or maybe not so free and full of life
But caught and trapped.
A trace of pulsing flesh
Becoming no more than a stain
A shape
A burnt out case
Reduced to naught
Eliminated.

I suffer no violence but
Perhaps the silhouettes hold more intensity than
One life slowly called to be a shadow.
To encounter the benign indifference of others
To watch eyes that look beyond not at me
To pass through conversation
That neither touches me
Nor was ever intended to.

Ineluctably I am drawn towards being both
Silhouette and shadow
Each sharing an inevitable sense of
Tragedy.

September-October 2007

6

RED DUST

Effortlessly invading my mouth
The finest grain of red soil grates as tooth
Meets tooth; I wonder how it slipped past lips
Squeezed tight. It troubles me that I cannot

Avert the gaze of young brown eyes that burn
Through dust-dulled skin. Or look at the faces
Where red dust has clotted glistening snot.
They brace themselves against the wind's fierce attack
Which stabs at eyes and skin like fine needles.
Bodies smudged together and lost in
A swirling cloud that demands no less than
Total oblivion. A shamble of

Huts are fashioned from this dust. Pushed and beaten
And pummeled to shape, they stand there for just
A while until they return to
The air to torment and humiliate
Those already broken. Later in the

Cool and quiet space of a room I bend
A finger to gently lift the finest
Grain of dust from my eye. A line of red
Has formed in the crease of the open book
I hold. I blow gently, then stop and stare
Unblinking
At the clean page.

August - November 2007

7

JAZZ NEEDS THE DARKNESS

As hard jewels spill from a soft pouch
So the notes come beautifully tumbling out.
Some stop to rest quickly
Others slip, slide, roll and fall.
Then there is stillness, where
Perfect balance quietly asserts itself
And each note exults in its place
Poised in a delicate constellation of sound.
Just as the stars need the blackest of nights
For the sky to surrender its subtlest rhythms
And for the eye to penetrate
The distant filigree of forms, so too
Jazz needs the darkness.

When the dazzling music pauses or breaks
I listen to the silences that settle
Into the spaces of nothingness where
Only God can be found. I hold on
To those exquisite moments, then weigh
Silence against blackness. The musicians
Exchange and breathe notes into the air like
Warm conversation
Eyes closed as if sight would blind them from the
Purest and clearest communication.
Just as jazz feels its way by reaching out and touching
So too I need the darkness.

November 2007

8

DATE FATE DAVE

Every time I search for Dave
I find Date and Fate.
Amusing at first, but now it's mantra-like:
Date Fate Dave Date Fate Dave Date Fate Dave.

Perhaps its repetition will transport
Me to a state of enlightenment
Of blissful detachment from all meaning
Date Fate Dave Date Fate Dave Date Fate Dave.

Perhaps serendipity has produced
An encrypted code.
Let me ponder for long enough and I'll find
My epiphany
Date Fate Dave Date Fate Dave Date Fate Dave.

Perhaps it's just a tic in the machine
Date Fate Dave caught forever in a loop
Of meaningless co-existence along with
Lips Kiss Lisp
Time Vine Wind
Book Cool Cook.

November 2007

AUTUMN TREE

The sun has burned a hole through the blue sky
And artfully composed itself in the long
Featureless window
In front of which I sit.

It has visited me in varying moods
Sometimes dressed in cloud
Or striking up a pose of thoughtful melancholy.
But after the best part of a year
Standing inconspicuous
Amongst the summer greens and winter browns
This autumn tree presses itself into my view.

Urgently and persistently it glows
And rattles
And whispers
And dances.
The sky can offer its coolest blue
Or its most leaden grey
But the flickering pendants of colour
Tune themselves against it
To create the purest harmony or most
Daring dissonance.

Finally with furious abandon
It weeps its leaves
And is gone
Leaving the sun to maintain a steady orbit.

November 2007

THE BRIDGE

The elegant gesture of cables and concrete
Flung without effort from bank to bank
In a taut geometry of beauty and daring;
Just as a piercing insight
Draws together two thoughts
Stranded each side of a chasm.

If you could only hear it
The cables
Each as thick as a human thigh
And strands of steel
As fine as a child's hair
Are quietly snapping
One by One.

I want to stand in the centre of that bridge
And let the mindless traffic rush by.
Then I will strain every unsnapped fibre of
My own to listen and
Wait for just that
Moment when cool construction first trembles
Then finally tumbles
Into the abyss.

March 2008

LEVITICUS

To see another life as an obstacle
Something to be erased
Meaningless and worthless;
That is an abomination.

To be so blind to Beauty that you
Crush it without knowledge or thought;
That is an abomination.

Not to act against the
Suffering on this earth;
That is an abomination.

Not to recognise the anger and hatred that
Hollows out every soul;
That is an abomination.

Not to feel shame at the cruel exercise of
Power and violence in and around us;
That is an abomination.

Not to celebrate any love expressed or
Exchanged in this world, no matter how
Imperfect or incomplete;
That is an abomination.

July 2008

NO MISTAKE (A DREAM)

I thought it might be a mistake to return
To feel the chill of those who wondered why
We'd met again.
For why do I seek friendly faces
When I sense I'll find none?
There is just torpor and
The settling of dust.

Too late to change my mind
I join an act of worship where we sit
And face the black and depthless void
That's sealed like a tightly closed window.

And then a crack as a bullet flies
And forms a perfect hole
Puncturing all that seemed dark and impenetrable.
I work it out that if I take the next seat
The one I'd planned for
The next bullet will hit me fair and square
Between the eyes.
No more to be done.

A pastoral voice murmurs
'It's being dealt with. There will be no more bullets.'
Then I carefully consider the angle again
And share none of this confidence.

July 2008

GENTLE THEFT

Just the other night my father's world was
Quietly and gently stolen.

With the superstitious regularity of old age
He laid down his body
Still not drained of vigour
And closed old eyes that had led him all day
To maintain a simple life.

What cruelty to be woken in the morning with the
Same gentleness of a mother waking a child
Yet to find his mind and limbs still intact
But his sight snatched away.

He sits in a chair
By a bed
In the corner
Of a sterile
Hospital ward
And looks ahead with the same blue eyes
As yesterday.

Turning to me he says
He will never see his face again.
Never see the garden whose colours and textures
He'd teased and encouraged from unwilling soil.
Never turn the pages of books and become lost
In their plots and intrigues.

Mind and limbs are poised like a dog waiting
To bound out into the day
Continuing to seek pleasure and meaning from life
But his glazed unfocused eyes shed tears
For a body and mind he will now
Only disappoint.

September 2008

HAILSTORM

Without warning
The innocent grey sky dashed us with
Hail so fierce that the moor could
Offer no protection.
Pearls of ice drove deep into our faces
And eyes were dented and hammered through
Paper-thin eyelids closed tight.

Yet unforced smiles appeared and through slightly
Opened mouths the hail found ways to
Batter and sting our teeth and gums.

We finally stood still as dead trees
Backs to the storm until it had passed.
Then with the weakest warmth of the sun
We gazed at a glittering world piled with icy pearls.

As the sun quickly grew stronger
Something compelled us to scoop up handfuls and
Fling them into each other's faces.
Laughing, and knowing all the time that
The growing warmth would soon
Rob us of this gift.

September 2008

16

TAGORE'S GITANJALI

Just inside the cover
Written with a neat hand
Reads E.R.C.N.B.W. 18.1.29.
When I get home and look more closely
I find many uncut pages
Words of joy and hope sealed up and
Unread by E.R.C.N.B.W.
Eighty two years ago.

I take a sharp knife
And with a sound like buttering toast
Gently slit open the pages of thick parchment.
At last words of
Blessing, longing and revelation are
Released into the sunlight like fragrant petals.

Sadly there were eighty two years
Where E.R.C.N.B.W remained
Unblessed or indifferent to
Tagore's passionate tones.

July 2011

WOLF

I press myself against the walls
And take comfort from the warmth of life within.
Grateful
I now turn towards the chill black night
Which tugs me back to its margins and spaces.
Here I look to a weightless sky above and a
Heavy earth below and weave a path
Between freedom and captivity.

Pursued or pursuing?
Frightened or frightening?
Brave or cowardly?
Friendly or friendless?
Purposeful or purposeless?

I envy the one with certainty who says,
'This is where I belong,
When I die take my heart and place it here.'
And the man who finds God and
Sews a carefully folded
Piece of parchment into his hem which reads:
'Joy, joy, joy, tears of joy.'

One dark night I'll tear down every street name
Every road sign
And watch at day break when things
Grind to a halt.
Not from malice
But to observe the absurd
To see what happens
When information and instructions
Cease.

Meanwhile
I continue to move on
Largely unobserved
Trying to create no slipstream
Leave no trace.

As I stand out here in the
Quiet wasteland there is a pleasing melancholy in
Turning my head to the sky and sending out a
Plume of cold breath,
Which blurs the stars for
Just a few seconds.

January 2009

WHITE POOL

Soft sunless spring warmth
Coaxing cool white petals
Tightly curled to
Push against furry bud cases
Until they split.

Now slim white fingers
Impatiently point
To stretch and gesture urgently
Until they explode from the tips
Luminous, bold and disheveled.

Each morning I have to look at them
A demanding presence
Fierce and unmitigated against
Leafless branches.
Staring wide-eyed like the faces of
Prophets carrying a heavy message
That must remain wordless.
There they withstand the wind and rain
With stoic acceptance.

Then as though one last
Visionary gesture is made
Or as if the burden of silence can
No longer be endured
White tears fall and settle
In a thick pool.
Is it a blessing
Or a curse?
To redeem or damn us?
There the tears remain
Too substantial to be displaced by an
Indifferent wind.

Very soon green leaves
Wriggle through to greedily
Soak up the hot summer sun
Unaware of the clotted white
Pool they stand in
Unaware that there could be
Anything but warmth and comfort
In their world.

March - April 2009

FIELD MOUSE

Trapped in my bin your
Future is finely balanced.
Slithering down the liner to
Reach your goal of breakfast's
Waste of toast and marmalade you
Had no thought of how useless
Pin-sharp claws would be to
Escape from a wall of
Slippery plastic.

I gently lift you up
Entombed
And stare at you staring at me.
Whiskers twitch in front of
Fierce dark beads for eyes and
Perfect glossy hairs cover your
Gently pulsing body.
This brings out a tenderness in me
Towards something
So perfectly made and
So easily crushed.
The tail curls in a calligraphic flourish
But its artistry is mocked from
Trailing through marmalade.

I kneel and gently tip up the bin.
A body which in one moment was inert
Awaiting its destiny
Now tumbles like a leaf being
Blown under a bush into
A world that opens up and enfolds it.

July 2009

UNDER A SALMON SKY

As I run
The heat rising from my head
Warms my hair and
I smell the sweet smoky wood
You burned last night
While we sat under a salmon sky
In a dusk that was warm and soft.

We breezed through light conversation
And then settled on deeper things
Tugging our chins and hair
Thoughtfully
Uncomfortably
Looking for ways of shedding some light.
Meanwhile,

Your sleek black cat
Threaded its way through the garden
Silently and effortlessly
Slipping past furniture, plants and people
But disturbing nothing.
Suddenly flashing its yellow eyes
From some unexpected point
Nearby or far away.

In this way it weaved together
Our conversation.
But all the time
Dusk turned to darkness
Until the cat was covered by night
And it was time for us to quietly leave.

July 2011

DENSE BLACK NIGHT (A DREAM))

A dense black night
And we need to pitch our tent
Somewhere amongst the others
Which rise from the ground
Like phantoms.

As I gaze a kingfisher lands
Between the cleft of two tents
Its orange and blue body
Flickering and sizzling
As though electrically charged
To light up the gloom.

Excitedly
I turn to my companion
But know he has seen nothing and
Now it is too late to share in
This miracle
Together.

December 2011

WAITING

A stool placed in the garden
So that my father can
Push his bony back against
The sun soaked wall.

Feeling the warmth
Enjoying the breeze
Thoughts beginning to surface
Though rarely to console.

His body is frail and stiff
As he forms an agitated right-angle
Caught between wall and stool.

'The trouble is I see nothing,'
He tells me
And I listen
Knowing
He is not talking about his eyes
Which only admit a shadowy world.

But with a melancholic resignation
He means his undug interior life:
Regrets
Vanished aspirations
Anxiety
A need for order
All boiling up against his will.

He takes a deep breath
Sighs
And says with hollow conviction
'Oh well we've got to keep going
Haven't we.'
I leave my question unasked:
'Going where, Dad?'

It is cold when he
Slowly rises each morning,
With his clothes laid out the night before.
Then his fingers are his eyes to find
Buttonholes and zips
And breakfast and the radio.
'Got to keep going,'
He says to himself.

July 2011

HOVERFLIES

Each day
Outside my garden door
Hoverflies busily flicker
With tireless persistence
Worrying the flaunting lilies and
Avoiding each other
Like high-speed helicopters
While they catch the pollen
From nodding anthers
And drink the sticky nectar.

What they draw in
Or take away from the lilies
Is a mystery to me
But I join them by bending low
And breathing in the heavily scented liquor
From the flowering cups.

Early this morning
In the quiet of the day
Before the sun had warmed the flowers
I see that last night
As the doors stayed open
Many hoverflies were lured
Into the conservatory
Which had kept until late
The warmth of the previous day.
They now lie on the windowsills.

Just a few feet away
The other side of the glass
Where lilies stand
And hoverflies gather for a fresh day
I hold one from yesterday in my palm
Then let it go in the wind
Where it drifts away
As easily as a husk.
Last night it exchanged the life-giving lily
For the warmth of a glass prison
And met with a comfortable death.

July 2011

YESTERDAY

I am a Muslim boy
And wear my Taquyah with pride.
Yesterday
My teacher said to me
'Why do you wear that skull cap?'
But meant no offence and
Even smiled benignly when he said it.
But
I burned inside
At his ignorant insult.

September 2011

30

FRUIT TREE

You have stood there for weeks
Holding out your tempting gift
Of bright swollen fruit
While I have given you scant attention.

Today
I work in the garden just
A short distance from you
And hear a hollow thump
As a fruit hits the ground.

My head turns sharply
To catch the rocking orb
Until it quietly sits there
Glowing.

It waits
Its task complete
It can do no more
It has entreated me long enough
This is my last chance
To acknowledge such abundance.

September 2011

SATURDAY AFTERNOON IN THE PARK

I stand
Held high in the small balcony
Of my friend's flat
With a glass of red wine
On the warmest of October afternoons where
Even so late in the day
The bland park below holds many
In its green palm.
Scattered and settled there
Less by choice than where
Gravity has pulled them.
Away from the dense noise
Of stifling streets.

Two girls face each other with
Small clouds of smoke rising between them
Like escaping thoughts.

Alone a man lays curled and motionless
And I wonder if his solitude
Is being enjoyed.

Groups of all sizes and ages
Clash with discordant clothes and clatter
With conversation
Food and drink.
Dogs and small children transgress
Wandering from group to group
Respecting no boundaries.

A rhythmic dull thud
Like the heartbeat of a place
Comes from a football being kicked
By a man with sunburned tattoos
To and fro
To and fro
Between a group of smiling friends.
And as if to challenge this imposed pulse and pace
The leisurely beat of a deep drum
Insinuates itself into the scene.

Suddenly the flash from a camera
Tries too hard to capture something
Which has been held together
With the lightest of touches.
And then a train zipping by
Conspires to erase this moment once and for all.

Still
I continue to stare at
A scene which had been held so perfectly
Even if only briefly
Detached from a driven world.

September 2011

JUPITER

It seems
That I have been
Chasing you for weeks.
But on reflection
I think you have been chasing me.

Your brightness has halted me
Many times
As you edged your way into
Each window frame I passed and
Every door I opened.

In my urban sky
You still managed to blaze away
Buried in a black void alone
But holding a steady gaze
Like a knowing eye.

Until,
Late one night
When I would have preferred sleep
You called to me silently and
Drew me closer.
You showed me the four
Bright moons
Which surround you like
Devoted acolytes.

For the first time I wondered
How I could have missed you before
Then realised
That I am only just beginning to sense the
Tug of the universe
Lifting me away
Almost imperceptibly
From the gravity of the earth.

I am beginning to glimpse
The mesmerising vastness of space
Which fills my eyes and lungs
Not with terror or loneliness but
With growing exhilaration as it
Gently and lovingly
Beckons me.

November 2011

GREY

A grey day
Grey mood
Grey dust
Grey cobwebs
As I tidy the shed.

Close to finishing
I walk away
Leaving an open door and
Glimpse a bird fly in.

A robin sits there and surveys
The scene
Just as he might
On the handle of a fork
When I rest from digging.

His presence has animated the greyness
With bright eyes
And alert twitching body
Searching for something here
Of interest.

I wait outside
Away from the door,
Almost out of respect
Recognising that for now
The shed is no longer my space.

After a while I see nothing different at first
But feel the slightest
Whisper of air
And know that he is gone
And the shed will resume its duty
Transformed.

November 2011

WALKING IN THE WINTER WIND

Groups of black crows hug trees
And haunt fields,
Occasionally
Provoked by the wind to
Sweep up into the sky
Only to return to their places
Like waves folding back to the shore.

My face feels the harsh scraping
Of a chill wind and
Dry leaves rush
Before my eyes
In a brittle and jagged dance.
But just a few months ago
Tempted by the warmth of the sun
It was butterflies
Who filled my vision;
Holding court in the air
Using the light breath of wind
For their dervish dances.

The place and time of nature's seasons
Cares not for what will console or
Comfort me
But the wind whispers
To patiently wait and see.

January 2012

PROMISE

A sharp cold day
Leads a sparrow to
Come close to my window
And fill its biil
With a plump red berry
Standing out vividly
Against the recent snow.

Another sits nearby
Tightly clasping a wisp
Of feather
Brandishing it as if to
Defy the hardships of winter and
Deny the satisfaction of bright berries
While dreaming instead of the
Warmth, softness and fecundity
Of spring.

Feb 2012

I IMAGINE A BALLOON

I imagine a balloon
Being lightly freed
From the hand of a child
Perhaps at a birthday party
And wonder if they smiled
As it was drawn upwards
Wishing they too could defy gravity.
Straining to see it disappear
Bobbing and lifting in currents of air
Worrying briefly that it may be
Halted by a tree
Before turning away
Distracted.

Held fast between leafless branches
Old plastic bags flap wildly as they
Become ribbons steadily torn
Sliver by sliver
To satisfy the wind's appetite.
And just occasionally
A bright deflated balloon
Is held there too
Like an exotic winter fruit
With a tail of ribbon still fluttering
Having failed in its effort
To journey forever.
It waits alongside the plastic bags
For the wind to do its
Annihilating work.

March 2012

40

SPRING PETALS

I love the new petals that
Slowly emerge in spring.
Since the winter has starved me
Of their touch
I now eagerly await
Each different flower to open.
Those that are cool and thick
As parchment;
Others soft and hanging heavy
With raindrops
Whose delicacy could be destroyed
Between thumb and finger.

I see the bees who
Show none of my detached pleasure but
Roughly push petals aside
To seek nourishment.

I watch the flowers moving
Gently in the breeze and
Observe the resistance different petals can offer.

I sit and consider my resistance
To the same breeze and think
How I would like to sway gently
Carrying the raindrops until
They slip away back to the earth.

March 2012

DREAM

It was a generous and gentle sleep,
Quite rare these days
Where events and thoughts
Tumbled over each other
With the delight of a game;
Where pleasure could be taken
From the ease of a movement
The lightness of a touch
A certain sense of fit.

Where all was unhurried
And reason withheld
Where things blossomed into a smile
And a confident ease
From looking at what was,
Not at what could
Or should be.

How far can I carry this into my day
Before I stop listening and seeing
Those smallest of moments
Which gather together
To hold meaning and purpose;
Things written down before my eyes
With a gossamer touch?

Until coarse words and actions
Seek once again to erase them,
Preferring gravity to grace.

May 2012

SWIFT BLACK LINE

Under a chalk blue sky
A blackbird draws a straight line
Between two fields straddling my path
One of pink grass
The other heavy heads of corn.

Although completed in a second
And no longer seen
It was that precise moment
On that exact day when
This configuration
Settled perfectly together
In union
Inscribed onto the landscape
Forever.

June 2012

43

IVY

Over the weeks
I've noticed the ivy
Wriggle its way through gaps unknown to me
To explore the inside of my shed.

Until this morning I'd watched its progress
With benign indifference
Finding satisfaction in the vigour
Of its enquiry.
With thick glossy leaves
Stout stem and eager fingers
Looking for the right object or surface
To tightly grip.

Why today did
I choose to challenge its journeying and
Cut it back?
Because it was blocking my way?
Or I could no longer bear its
Audacious invasion of my space?

What would I have learned if I had left it?
How to caress the handle of a fork?
How to span spaces like an acrobat?
How to slip effortlessly across a room?
How worthwhile it is to reach out
With the most tentative of searching,
Trusting that before long a firm hold will
Offer itself?

July 2012

44

CURIOUS COMPANIONS

On a night when little sleep comes
My mind fills with dark
Heavy thoughts fierce
Enough to keep away the
Warm embrace that night extends.

I look with staring, stinging eyes
At the wall ahead where
Parading in front of me
Are the shadows of the traffic
From nine floors below.
A slow procession of silent phantoms
Each different in size or brightness
Offering curious companionship
With only the sound of a horn to remind me
That people still exist among the shadows.

October 2012

GRAVITY

My kittens spin and twist
Balancing precariously on objects
That will certainly fail them.
But they are drawn by a spontaneity
That doesn't pause to
Consider consequences.
When slipping and falling
As they do
Their bright eyes blink
Bodies flick back
To stand
Shake themselves
And start again.

My father is old
He ties his shoelaces standing
On one leg
Loses his balance
Pirouettes
And falls.
Painfully
And slowly
He stands.
Later in the day he rolls up his sleeve
And shows me his arm
Bruised to the colour of burgundy wine.
Toying with gravity as kittens do
Punishes him
Severely.

March 2013

STARS AND RIVERS

Through the skylight above my head
As I lay in bed
Several stars punctuate the sky
As they have done for
Several nights now
Extending their
Steady watch
From light years away
While outside my window the
Afon Ysgir
Rushes and gurgles by
Carrying the world in motion.

I need do nothing
But feel the space and closeness
Between steady stars and rushing rivers
And take my sleep.

May 2013

THE WIND'S WORK

To feel the wind
Full in my face
With open hills around
I remind myself that it

Calls me
Ruffles me
Exhausts me
Exhilarates me
Cools and warms me
Animates the trees and
Sings and whistles to me
Delivered and drives me
Curls and twists the clouds
Around me
And one day
I pray it will gently
And lovingly
Carry me away.

May 2013

AGAINST DARKNESS

All week I have found
Beautiful, fragile moments
Of our time spent together
And guarded them
Like warm eggs in a
Soft moss-lined nest.

But this morning
In that vulnerable moment
Just as I awoke
I allowed in what
Loves to extinguish light.

Now all is hidden from me
And without love
I turn to others
Finding a world that moves
But does not live.

I need light before I can make
Another move.
For that I have to call out
Into the bloodless morning
For what will
Strengthen me against darkness.

May 2013

MEMENTO MORI

Fear and resignation
Linger
In an atmosphere thick and chilling
Choking endless corridors.

Barely space left
For the bewildered and angry
Who stalk this labyrinth
Looking at signage
Looking for food and coffee
But finding nothing.

You expect
To see mortality inscribed
In the eyes
And on faces and bodies of the frail
Being wheeled along on trolleys and chairs
Like some macabre carnival procession.

But I see it too
In the brisk stride of visitors
Imagining themselves
Immune from absorption into this
Blood full
Bloodless
Place.

Now it is late and
I am still here.
The corridors have emptied of people but
For a solitary cleaner
Dwarfed by white space
Who lifts her mop like a weapon
And targets two bright drops of blood
On the floor.

Doctors with stethoscopes
Appear and disappear
Spectre-like
Between rooms and corridors
Moving purposefully and
Confident in the knowledge
Perhaps reluctantly
That they are designated
As custodians
Of this chilling system that
Processes sickness and death.

May 2013

BUNTING

The softest and finest
Strands of sheep wool
Snagged by the barbed wire fence
Something so light and weightless
For the wind to carry
Yet trapped so easily
By the tip of a spike
Flailing and flapping
In irregular rows
Left like delicate bunting to
Line each side of my walk
Through this narrow road
Between gentle Welsh hills.

May 2013

UNIVERSES

While we gaze out at
Dim and distant galaxies
Searching for meaning and purpose
My kittens lay down and stare
Into the dark deep narrow space
Underneath the freezer
Peering and pawing
For whatever they may find
To toy with
To chew
To chase
With wide-eyed wonder
Equal to ours.

May 2013

JEWELS

Raindrops strike the window
Like bullets
Then gather
Into swollen droplets
Which meander
Erratically
Downwards.

Wide-eyed
The kittens' paws reach out
To trap just one jewel
As it speeds away
Heads twitching in indecision
Wondering which to follow.
But each effort proves futile
While they sit
On the dry side
Of the glass.

I watch the glistening drops
Being covered by
Confident paws
And see their surprise
As the jewels elude them
And slip away,
As they always will.

June 2013

54

FULLNESS

You drank
From the pale lilac flowers
With your paper-thin wings
Silently clapping in the sun
While surrounded by
Bustling bees
Seeking the same nectar.

I had been thinking of fullness
While harvesting salad leaves
Before breakfast but
Remained unable to grasp
What it might mean or feel like.

Yet here I saw the source of fullness
Being gently sipped
Simply and
Completely.

July 2013

GLENN

Shortly before you died
You wrote
Glenn
Glenn
Glenn
Glenn
Over and over again
In Pete's diary
Like a boy affirming his identity or
Practising writing autographs
Before he becomes famous.

But
You were a man and maybe writing your name
Was one thing that held you together
Proved that you still existed.
You were built
For tough physical work
You charmed
You sported the classic scar across your cheek
Suggesting a dark and interesting past.
You were a soldier in Afghanistan.

But
You were also an alcoholic and
Drug addict.
And
Even as you wrote Glenn
Over and over again
You were dissembling
Disintegrating.

In a tent
On some wasteland
You completed what you had no
Strength to resist
You died from an overdose
You wanted to be Glenn
But it was never to be
Now you are just
G
L
E
N
N
Each letter having fled
Back to formlessness
Just as you were struggling to
Wrestle them together
Hoping you might stand a chance of
Continuing to live and breathe
As Glenn.

August 2013

NO ANSWER

After his stroke
My dad senses his
Mortality more acutely
Than ever
And says:
'The trouble is I never know if
I'm going to wake up
In the morning.'

I have no answer but
The trite reply that
It's the same for everyone.

Having just returned from
Many miles on the motorway
I recall the frequent black traces
Where rubber had twisted its
Distressed path towards
The hard shoulder.
Each track holding the story of
A journey stopped short
Suddenly
Unexpectedly
While other traffic
Flowed by ceaselessly
Hungry for more miles.

Why does my mind seek metaphors
Instead of finding words of consolation?

July 2013

RYOKAN

One table
Barely a metre square
Behind a window
In a cabin
Where I
Eat
Draw
Read
Think
Write and look,
As the trees sway and the
Birds and rabbits
Forage and move on.
I watch the rain and hear it
Dance on the thin roof.
See the sun and
Feel its warmth.
Gaze at the moon as it slips past
Each evening.
As a gift
On my final night
It forms a perfect disc
In the centre of my window.

I step out onto the verandah and
Deeply breathe in the moon's clear light
Until I am full
And then reach out my arms
Until I can stretch no further.

Sept 2013

59

CAT'S WHISKER

I picked out the cats' route
Narrow
Economical
Targeted
Cutting through dew-soaked grass:
From kitchen door to
Concrete path
At the bottom of the garden.
Used by them time after time
Stepped on like tight-rope walkers
Never looking down.
Then at the end
Their chosen direction remains unknown to me.

Looking like a long white trail
I picked up a cat's whisker
Shed on the floor.
Running my finger
From one stout end until it
Beautifully tapered away
Imperceptibly
To nothing.
There my thumb and finger met again
Skin against skin.

October 2013

SILENTLY EVEN AS I SLEEP

Silently
Even as I sleep
The tomatoes in my garden
Ripen from green to red,
Chillies grow plump,
Figs soften and brown,
Buds of Morning Glory prepare
Themselves to open like
Dazzling blue parasols.

Dewdrops jewel-like
Hang from leaves and
Cling to grass-blades.
Slugs and snails
Leave glistening trails.
Petals topple like tears from
My favourite rose.

The moon slips away
The sun rises
Nothing has waited for me
To open my eyes
Before changing.

September 2011 – May 2014

BRIEF LIFE

Today
When you flashed excited eyes at me
It was clear you had caught something.

I cupped the weightless bird that
Had been playfully interrogated
Soft and perfectly formed
So close to being fully sparrow.

Standing transfixed I watched
While your fledgling eyes slowly blinked
And body gently rose and fell
Breathing the same air as me.
Until suddenly

Your eyelids slipped closed and
All was still.
I dug a hole under a bush
Quite deep as though burying
A precious treasure.

Placing you there
The delicate shades of grey were
Lost against the cold brown soil.
So I found a marigold to lay beside you
Which glowed like the sun.

Then I stood and looked
Before pushing back the earth to cover
Something that had touched life
As lightly as one of its downy feathers
Had brushed my hand.

July/August 2014

IN THE CLASSROOM

A quiet voice
Speaks out against a riotous background
To ask the burning question
Hidden by others.
'So if life is nothing but suffering
And death is the end, what's the point?'
Her thirteen year old eyes look up to me
For an answer.

Even if it wasn't for the noise
Which clouds my mind
My space to pause and reflect
Has shut down.
My hands and face are a show of confusion
My eagerness to console scatters my thoughts
So I try to gently send her
Back to sit down
With well-worn words
And no answer.

February-September 2014

UNSEEN

How often do we miss the
Breath of an angel
Kissing our neck;

Or notice the silken
Movement of air
As they brush past us;

Or discover a smile that lifts our spirits
While wondering from
Where the gift came;

Or ponder on how we are comforted by a word
Heard quietly in a dream
Or uttered silently to our soul;

Or feel a delicate touch not on our skin
But somewhere deeply within
And out of reach?

There is a longing for us to lose ourselves
That we might find them
But again and again they graze our consciousness
Without us even knowing.

October 2014

GRACE

Thick cloying morning
Stuck beneath a heavy weight
But drop down to the river and
The world is translated.

Fish weave through the current
Patterning the depths.
Ducks meander
Lazily dipping.
Cormorants dive with clear intent.
Water bubbles down a weir
With the endless rhythm of vitality.
Then an egret cuts a slow
Beautiful line
Close and parallel to the water
Wings slowly and effortlessly
Measuring their pace to the river.
A grey heron sits on a rock in the centre
Like a sage sentinel
Motionless apart from an
Occasional twist of the head.

I am changed.
What has this brief descent brought me?
Movement
Fluidity
Lightness
The merest glimpse of a harmony
Which is forever present
And waiting to be discovered
Over and over again
So that we might be lifted.

October 2014

BOWING DEEPLY

The most inoffensive of hums begins
As the mechanism lowers
Another laden coffin
To the furnace below
Burning it to ashes.
But in this particular box
Is my father.

Everyone present was held in a
Brief moment of inertia
While they experienced finality.
Except me.
I bowed deeply to him
But never quite understood why,
Apart from a vague though sincere
Compulsion to express
Respect and farewell.

I learned in Japan today
That the deep bow can signify
Both respect and apology.
Now I realise that my
Body knew more than my
Mind could comfortably reconcile.
It had gracefully come to my aid
And I am left grateful
For the times when the reflexes of my body
Compensate for the dark confusion of my mind.

February-October 2014

THINGS BEST LEFT TO BE

As a child
I stood in awe watching butterflies
Iridescent and weightless commanding the air.
I captured some and
Pinned them in cases with fastidious attention.
Only to find I had lost what I loved.

Today I experienced the touch
Of a delicate spirit
And searched for words
To tell you about it.
Now I know I should have left it alone
To come and go
Wordlessly.

November 2014

BLACK RAIN

Kojiro Watanabe.
I have seen how both you and your pocket-watch
Stopped dead
At 8.15 on August 6th 1945
When black rain began to fall.

A sandstone head of Buddha
Seared of all features.
A small crooked stack of family tea bowls
Baked together inseparably.
Fine sewing needles fused into a pointless lump.
Glass bottles melted into lolling forms.
And the black rain fell.

School children fled home
In shredded clothes and burning skin
Soon to die.
A lock of singed hair is cut off
As evidence that a daughter once lived.
A mother keeps some nails and skin from her son
To show a father when he returns from war.
And the black rain fell.

Searching
For a son outside riding his tricycle
Finding
Both grotesquely robbed of play forever.
Searching
For her daughter
Finding
A wooden sandal with straps
Made from her kimono, holding the
Silhouetted shape of a young foot
Scorched there by the blast.
Searching
For a son who was heading for school
Finding
A lunchbox with its charred contents
Underneath his body
And the black rain fell.

This morning I pulled aside the curtains.
Marmalade sunlight poured in
Against a summer sky
Barely touched by cloud.
Yet still the black rain falls
Into thick puddles which reflect
The depth of our dark souls as they
Connive new dance steps
To death's tune.

October-November 2014

SHADOWY PLACES

I prefer the shadowy places
Beneath the trees
Where flowers don't pierce your eyes
With exuberant colour
Or sway together in a mass of
Warm summer revelry.

Inside the damp dark wood
There is a smell of sweet decay
Delicate blooms gather together
Where motes of light
Feed their needs and
Dark thick leaves force themselves
To where they can catch sun
Enough for even darker days.

Sinewy and determined
They patiently await the
Warmth and light
That will eventually come.

August –November 2014

FISH MARKET

At dawn
Looking down from my hotel room
To the Japanese garden below
The pond is full of plump carp.
There a white egret picks its way carefully
Around the edges and
Shoots out a long neck
To effortlessly spear smaller fish from
An abundant supply.

Here life and death are joined together in a scene
Which bind beauty and necessity.

I later stood in the vast fish market
Looking at all that had been
Robbed from the sea and where
Only the smell of death and profit linger.

November 2014

SILVER BIRCH

Silhouetted against the slate grey sky
Where long thin branches sway like hair
Large black birds perch.
Choosing stouter limbs they
Are strung out in a line;
Some in clusters
Others alone.
Occasionally one or two shift
As if to finely tune their position.
Together they sit like notes on
Some arcane stave
Waiting to be played
By unknown instruments.
And then
Suddenly disturbed
They are swept away
Along with their
Unplayed manuscript.

December 2014

CONIFER

A tired conifer
I thought
Continually shedding itself
To encrust everything beneath
In rusty brown needles
Or drooping its branches to catch me
As I walked down the garden path.

Today in winter
It is transformed
By a flock of goldfinches
Bobbing up and down
Flickering red and yellow
As they gorge on the seeds that
Simply wait for them.

I see the tree anew as
A provider
Rich with plenty and promise
And feel regret
That I only left it there
Because it conveniently
Hid the shed.

December 2014

TATTOOED

Relaxed by rum
He still searches me with fierce blue eyes
Set into sharp features
Shaved head and
A handsome face betrayed by
A smile which show
Ill-fitting false teeth
Courtesy of a feckless stepfather
When he was fourteen.

Homeless and
In the shelter;
Just out of jail;
Still buoyed by rum and Christmas;
He pulls off his shirt
To proudly show his tattoos.

Not sophisticated sleeves and designs
But a raw testament
Like pages torn from a diary
Scattered over his body to hold memories.
He places a finger on a swallow and smiles
'My dad took me to have this done when I was
fourteen. I got kicked out of school.'
He rests a hand on his heart
To cover the names of his two daughters
And declares his love for them.

Across from his heart is a faded winged tiger:
'Just took my fancy.'
His arms hold the names of girl friends.
His back has a cartoon bulldog
And the names Dan and Tom,
One on each shoulder blade:
Unskilfully etched in prison using ink
Blown from a biro and a needle
Sterilised over a flame.

He wanted to kill his stepfather
But he died anyway.
He loved his mother
But wasn't let out for her funeral.
Now he visits the grave each day
To talk to her.
'Tonight I am happy,' he says.

December 2014

STRANGE CHILD

A strange child for many reasons.
At 18
Church youth group.
I tell them:
Jung said he didn't know if he was sitting on a rock
Or whether he was the rock he was sitting on.
Brilliant I thought. Didn't know why
But knew it was brilliant.
I met silence in return
Then normal conversation resumed.

Many decades have passed
And this quote
Clung to my memory
Like a plant waiting to blossom.
Now it has flowered.
Brilliant I think.
I tell others
And meet inscrutable smiles in return,
Before normal conversation resumes.

December 2014

CATHEDRAL

It is a spring day
Warmed by a sun that
Cajoles the landscape
To slowly ripen
Towards summer.

My path is a solitary one
Through fields and scattered trees,
Drawn by a soothing drone.
I walk on
Alert to the growing sound until
Ahead of me
Standing alone in splendour
Is the glowing white canopy of
A hawthorn bush.

I climb beneath and
Stand by the trunk
Gazing with wonder at hundreds of bees
Heavy with pollen
Working above my head.
Pure in the activity and energy
Of what is given and taken.

To climb out again
Is like leaving a cathedral
After being struck with awe by its
Transcendental yet
Fragile architecture.

December 2014

FINDING YOU

Let me come to you on
Nightingale floorboards
So that my arrival is
Accompanied by bird song;

Even though I deserve no more
Than to creep in like a
Cheap thief
Stumbling on boards that creak.

December 2014

END OF THE DAY

White doves on the roof
Beached and washed up
Waiting for night's cover.

Three swans stretch out their necks
And cross a swollen dusk sky
That spares a strip of orange warmth
For flights of passage.

A black tower of cloud sits
Beside a fragile church spire.

Then
Night consumes them all.

December 2014

Made in the USA
Charleston, SC
03 March 2015